Friends

Robert was in Hill Street
with his mummy.
He saw a milk lorry.
He saw a police car.
He saw a little car
and a big bus.

Robert saw the policeman going into the shop.
The policeman got milk and a paper at the shop.
Robert got a comic at the shop.

A big lorry was going
along the street.
The driver saw Robert
and his mummy.
He stopped his lorry for them.

3

Robert saw a green van
and a yellow van.
The green van was big
but the yellow van was little.
It was the ice cream van.

The driver stopped
her ice cream van and
Robert got a big ice cream.
He went home
with his ice cream
and his comic.

Karen saw the ice cream van.
She said:
　Stop.
But the van did not stop.
Tommy's mummy saw it
and she said:
　Stop.
The driver stopped for them.
Karen and Tommy got ice cream.

The green van was a shop.
Robert saw it going
along the street.
Robert's mummy stopped it and
she got bread and milk.
Robert got a lollipop
from the driver.

Robert went to post
a postcard to his aunt.
He went along the street
and he posted the postcard.

The teacher came along the street.
She stopped at the pillar box
and she posted a letter.
Robert said:
   I posted a postcard
   to my aunt.

Robert saw the postman.

He was in a red van.

The postman stopped the van
at the pillar box
and he got the letters out.

He got Robert's postcard too.

Robert said his postcard was for his aunt.
He said it had little bears on it.
He said his aunt liked little bears.

It was Robert's birthday.

He was five.

He saw the postman going along the street.

The postman was reading the name on a letter.

It was Robert's name.

The postman came to Robert's house
and Robert got a birthday card.
It had a big 5 on it.
It had

Happy Birthday.

It had Robert's name on it too.
Robert's birthday card was
red and green and yellow.
It was from Karen.

Robert got ice cream
on his birthday and
he got a birthday present
in a box.
The box had his name on it.
It was from his mummy and daddy.
The box had cars in it.
It had green cars and
yellow cars and a big police car.

Robert went to play with his cars.

Karen and Tommy came
to see his present.
Karen said:
   Happy birthday Robert.
Tommy said:
   Happy birthday Robert.
Robert let them play with his cars.

Robert said:

   I am five.

   I am a big boy

   and I am going to school

   with Karen and Tommy.

Robert was happy on his birthday.

Tommy's mummy is going
to her work.
She is going in the bus.
She works in a shop
in Hill Street.
Tommy is with her and
he is going to school.

Tommy's mummy is in her shop.
A little boy is going to get
a birthday card.
A bus driver is
in the shop too and
he is going to get a paper.

Karen's daddy is at his work.

He is a policeman.

He is the driver in a police car.

He is reading the name
on a big van.

Tommy's mummy stopped work
at five o'clock.
She got bread and milk
at the shops
and she went home for tea.
Tommy had tea with his mummy
and he went out
to play with Karen.

Karen's daddy stopped work
at five o'clock.
He came home in the police car
and he had his tea.
He saw Tommy and Karen
playing in the park.

One day
Karen and Gary saw Robert
playing in his yellow car.
They liked his car and
they went to play with him.

Gary said:
   Stop.
   I am a policeman.
Robert stopped his car
and he got out.
Gary went into it.
Robert said:
   Get out of my car.
But Gary went away with it.

Karen stopped Gary and
she got into the yellow car.
Robert came and said:
 Get out of my car.
But Karen went away with it.
She did not see a big box
and she bumped into it.
She got out and she said:
 I'm going home.
She went home to her daddy.

Robert got his car back
and he said:
 I'm going home too.
He stopped playing and
he went home with his car.
Gary went to play by himself.

One day
the big green van came
along the street and
it stopped at Tommy's house.
Tommy's mummy said
she was going for bread
and Tommy went with her.

The driver had lollipops
in a box.
Tommy got a red one for himself.
His mummy said:
   Get a lollipop for Karen too.
So Tommy got a green one
for her.

Tommy had a birthday card to post.

So he went to a pillar box with Karen.

He was going to post his lollipop but Karen stopped him.

She said:

   Post the birthday card, not the lollipop.

Tommy posted the birthday card
and they went home
to Tommy's house.
He said to his mummy:
 I was going to post my lollipop
 but Karen stopped me.
His mummy said he was
a silly boy.

One day
Karen was going home and
she saw a letter on the street.
It had a name on it.
The letter was for Tommy's mummy.
Karen went to Tommy's house
with it.
But Tommy's mummy was not
at home.

So Karen went to her shop
with the letter.
But Tommy's mummy was
not at her work.
The girl in the shop said:
   She went to the play park
   with Tommy.

Karen came out of the shop.
She did not see Tommy
and his mummy
in the play park.
But she saw them
at the bus stop.
Tommy's mummy was happy
to get her letter back.
They went home for tea.